UNIT 3
BOOK 1

SRA Open Court Reading

Science Cycles

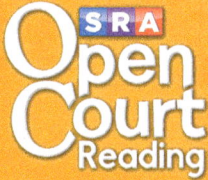

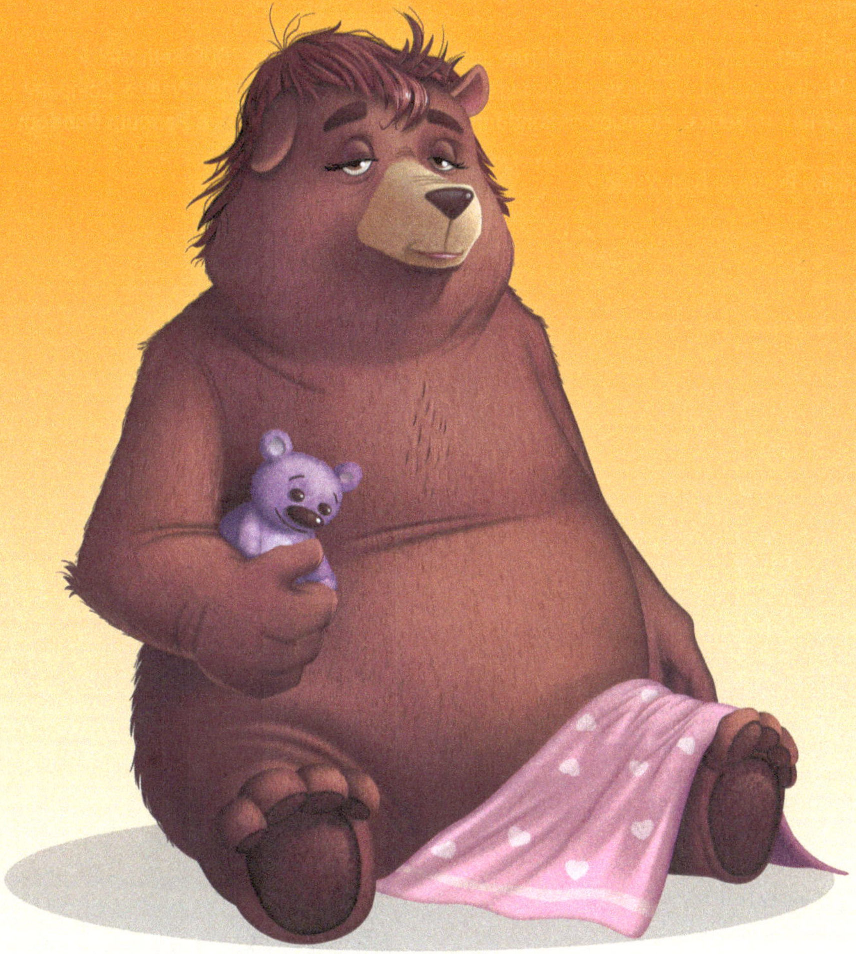

Grade 1

McGraw Hill Education

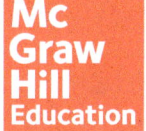

Program Authors

Carl Bereiter, Ph.D.
Andrew Biemiller, Ph.D.
Joe Campione, Ph.D.
Doug Fuchs, Ph.D.
Lynn Fuchs, Ph.D.

Steve Graham, Ph.D.
Karen Harris, Ph.D.
Jan Hirshberg, Ed.D.
Anne McKeough, Ph.D.
Marsha Roit, Ed.D.

Marlene Scardamalia, Ph.D.
Marcy Stein, Ph.D.
Gerald H. Treadway Jr, Ph.D.

Photo Credits

4 Raimund Linke/Photodisc/Getty Images; **5** tBoyan/E+/Getty Images, tBoyan/E+/Getty Images, tBoyan/E+/Getty Images; **52** Corey Hochachka/DesignPics, Alfonso de Tomas/Alamy; **53** Ken Cavanagh/McGraw-Hill Education.
Back Cover: tBoyan/E+/Getty Images, tBoyan/E+/Getty Images, tBoyan/E+/Getty Images.

Acknowledgments

Grateful acknowledgment is given to the following publishers and copyright owners for permissions granted to reprint selections from their publications. All possible care has been taken to trace ownership and secure permission for each selection included. In case of any errors or omissions, the Publisher will be pleased to make suitable acknowledgments in future editions.

"Excerpted from *Time Is When* by Beth Gleick, illustrated by Marthe Jocelyn. Text Copyright© 2008 Beth Gleick. Illustrations Copyright© 2008 Marthe Jocelyn. Originally published in the United States by Rand McNally & Company, 1960. Reprinted by permission of Tundra Books, a division of Random House of **Canada Limited, a Penguin Random House Company.**"
Reprinted with permission from the Estate of Beth Y. Gleick.

The Months by Sara Coleridge

MHEonline.com

Copyright © 2016 McGraw-Hill Education

All rights reserved. No part of this publication may be reproduced or distributed in any form or by any means, or stored in a database or retrieval system, without the prior written consent of McGraw-Hill Education, including, but not limited to, network storage or transmission, or broadcast for distance learning.

Send all inquiries to:
McGraw-Hill Education
8787 Orion Place
Columbus, OH 43240

ISBN: 978-0-07-667988-1
MHID: 0-07-667988-8

Printed in the United States of America.

7 8 9 BRP 24 23

UNIT 3 Science Cycles

Book 1

Table of Contents

Unit Overview 4

Time Is When 6
by Beth Gleick
illustrated by Marthe Jocelyn

The Months 30
by Sara Coleridge
illustrated by Teagan White

Jake's Tree 34
by Dennis Fertig
illustrated by Ziyue Chen

Glossary 52

UNIT 3 | Science Cycles

BIG Idea

What is a cycle?

Theme Connections

What cycle is shown here?

Background Builder Video
connected.mcgraw-hill.com

Essential Question What measurements of time can you think of?

Time Is When

by Beth Gleick
illustrated by Marthe Jocelyn

Time is from before to now; from now to later.

Time is seconds, minutes, hours, days, weeks, months, and years.
Time ticks by on clocks and watches.

Time moves on through pages on calendars. Time is when.

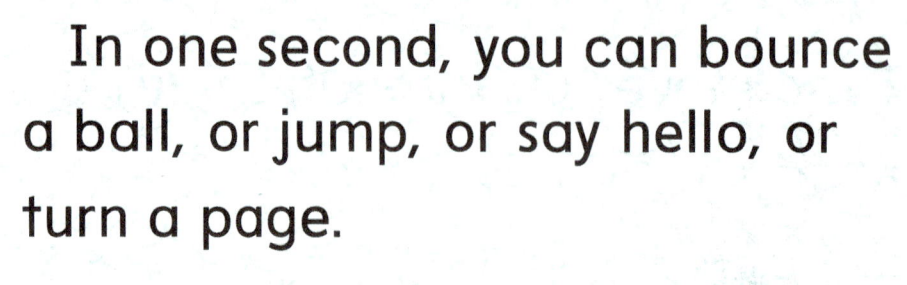
In one second, you can bounce a ball, or jump, or say hello, or turn a page.

A minute has 60 seconds.

In one minute, you can walk one block (if you walk quickly and don't stop to look in the store windows).

An hour has 60 minutes.

In one hour, you can paint a picture or build a make-believe city.

A day has 24 hours. It starts at midnight, while you are sleeping. It has a morning, a noon, an afternoon, and an evening.

And then it ends at midnight, again while you are sleeping.

In one day, you can do many things. Sometimes you do the same things every day; sometimes you do different things.

In a morning, you can get up out of bed, eat breakfast, and go to school.
At noon, you can eat lunch. In an afternoon, you can swing and climb and ride.

In an evening, you can eat supper and read a book, or watch television. At night, you sleep. While you are sleeping, a new day begins.

There are seven days in a week. From Sunday until the next Sunday is one week. There are about four weeks in one month and 52 weeks in one year.

A year has 12 months and four seasons.
From January until the next January is one year.

In some parts of the world, the start of the New Year is winter — trees without leaves, cold weather, and snow.

The spring months are often windy, warm, and rainy. The grass turns green, trees sprout leaves, flowers bloom, and birds sing.

In many places, the summer months have bright sunshine and crashing thunderstorms. Summer is usually a good time for boating, swimming, and fishing.

The fall months have cooler weather. The leaves turn red, yellow, and brown, and the wind blows them off the trees. It is the end of another year.

From your last birthday to your next birthday is one year. In the many seconds, minutes, hours, days, weeks, and months that make up one year, you can do many things.

But most important of all, you grow one year older.

The time past is yesterday, and all of the days, weeks, months, and years that are behind you. The time now, the present time, is today — this hour, this minute, this second.

The future time is tomorrow, and all of the days, weeks, months, and years that are ahead of you.

Time is from before to now; from now to later. Time is when.

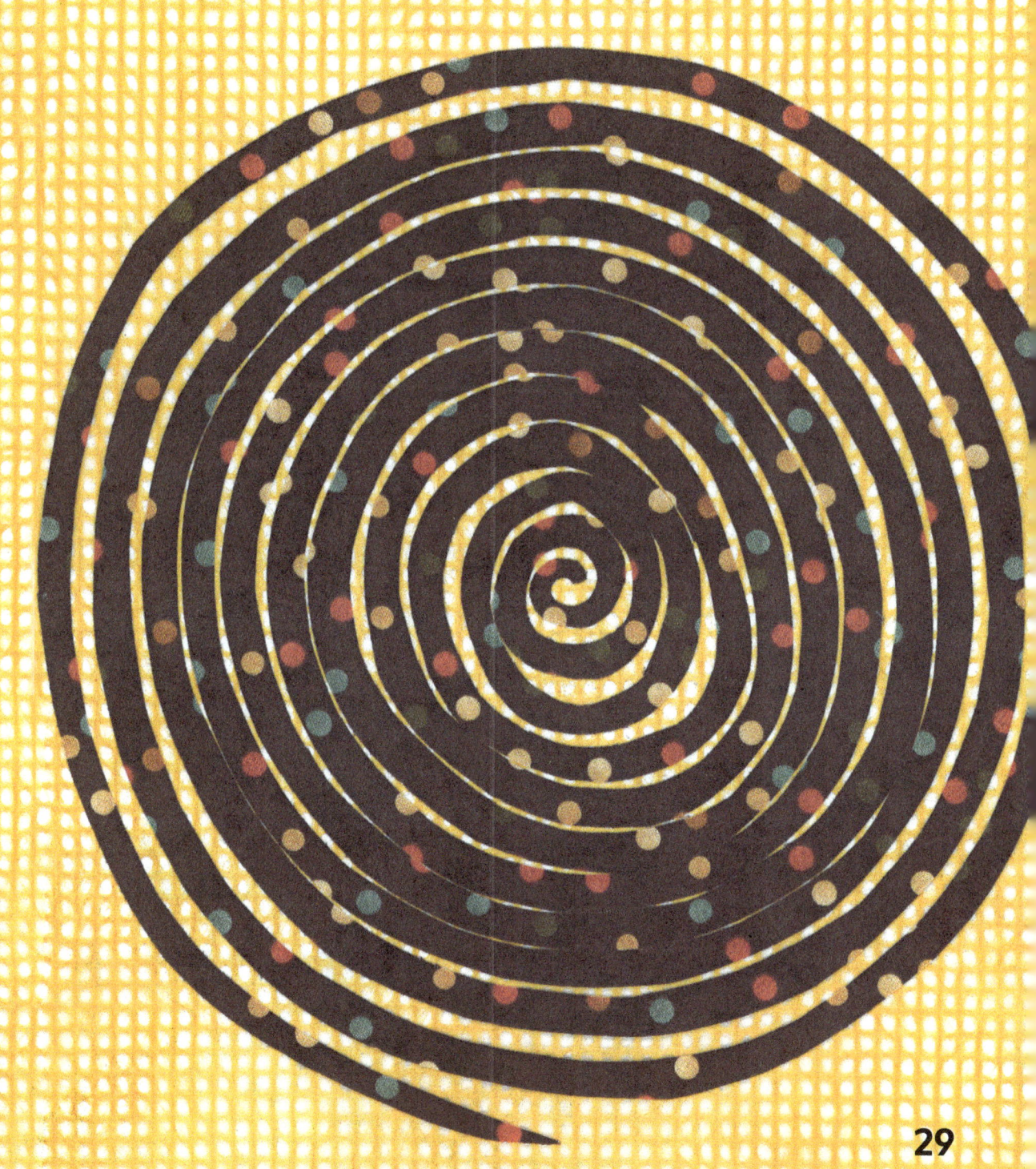

Essential Questions What is your favorite time of year? Why do you like it?

The Months

by Sara Coleridge
illustrated by Teagan White

January brings the snow,
Makes our feet and fingers glow.

February brings the rain,
Thaws the frozen lake again.

March brings breezes loud and shrill,
Stirs the dancing daffodil.

April brings the primrose sweet,
Scatters daisies at our feet.

May brings flocks of pretty lambs,
Skipping by their fleecy dams.

June brings tulips, lilies, roses,
Fills the children's hands with posies.

Hot July brings cooling showers,
Apricots and gillyflowers.

August brings the sheaves of corn,
Then the harvest home is borne.

Warm September brings the fruit,
Sportsmen then begin to shoot.

Fresh October brings the pheasants,
Then to gather nuts is pleasant.

Dull November brings the blast,
Then the leaves are whirling fast.

Chill December brings the sleet,
Blazing fire, and winter treat.

Essential Question What changes in nature can you see?

Jake's Tree

by Dennis Fertig
illustrated by Ziyue Chen

Jake looked out at the gray winter sky. He studied a tall tree in the yard.

The tree did not have any leaves. Snow covered its branches. Snow covered the ground around it.

Strong winds shook the tree's branches. The tree looked like it was shivering! Could it feel cold?

On paper, Jake printed, "A tall tree shivers on a cold winter day."

He pinned the paper on his wall.

Two months later, it was early spring. Yet it was still cold and some snow had not melted.

Jake slipped on his winter coat. He went outside to hunt for signs of spring.

Jake felt cold raindrops on his face. But he spotted buds on the tree. They would grow into green leaves!

Jake wrote another sentence and pinned it on the wall. "In spring, the tree's buds promise a warm, green May."

It was summer at last! Jake loved hot weather and sunny skies. He even loved warm summer rain.

At times, gentle summer breezes blew through the tree. That almost sounded like waves at the ocean.

In the heat, Jake liked the tree's cool shade. He and his friends played under the big tree.

He wrote another sentence for the wall. "All summer, the big tree shades us as we play."

But summer cannot last.
Jake didn't mind too much.
A beautiful fall was nice too.

He enjoyed the smells of a cool fall evening. He liked the feel of a warm sweater.

Jake had watched red, brown, and gold leaves fill the branches. Then they filled the yard!

Jake wrote another sentence. "In fall, the tree's leaves slowly drift away."

Jake read his poem on the wall.

A tall tree shivers on a cold winter day.

In spring, the tree's buds promise a warm, green May.

All summer, the big tree shades us as we play.

In fall, the tree's leaves slowly drift away.

Glossary

A

ahead
into the future

B

before
at an earlier time

bloom
to grow and produce flowers

bud
a small part that grows on a plant and develops into a flower, leaf, or new branch

C

calendar
a chart showing the days, weeks, and months of a year

covered
a form of the verb **cover**: to put something over it

H

hour
60 minutes; one of 24 equal parts of the day

M

melted
a form of the verb **melt**: to gradually become less

midnight
the middle of the night, specifically 12 o'clock

S

season
one of the four quarters into which the year is commonly divided

shook
a form of the verb **shake**: to move back and forth with quick movements

studied
a form of the verb **study**: the process of learning

T

through
by means of